T0149476

The *Loving* ROAD to TRUTH

DORIS FOURACRE

BALBOA
PRESS
A DIVISION OF HAY HOUSE

Balboa Press books may be ordered through booksellers or by contacting:

Balboa Press
A Division of Hay House
1663 Liberty Drive
Bloomington, IN 47403
www.balboapress.com
1 (877) 407-4847

Because of the dynamic nature of the Internet, any web addresses or
links contained in this book may have changed since publication and
may no longer be valid. The views expressed in this work are solely those
of the author and do not necessarily reflect the views of the publisher,
and the publisher hereby disclaims any responsibility for them.

The author of this book does not dispense medical advice or prescribe the use
of any technique as a form of treatment for physical, emotional, or medical
problems without the advice of a physician, either directly or indirectly. The
intent of the author is only to offer information of a general nature to help
you in your quest for emotional and spiritual well-being. In the event you use
any of the information in this book for yourself, which is your constitutional
right, the author and the publisher assume no responsibility for your actions.

Any people depicted in stock imagery provided by Thinkstock are
models, and such images are being used for illustrative purposes only.
Certain stock imagery © Thinkstock.

Print information available on the last page.

ISBN: 978-1-5043-9058-3 (sc)
ISBN: 978-1-5043-9118-4 (e)

Library of Congress Control Number: 2017916627

Balboa Press rev. date: 10/25/2017

Contents

Chapter 1 — Letting Go..1

Chapter 2 — Reincarnation: Another Way...................9

Chapter 3 — What Is This Thing Called Love?..........16

Chapter 4 — The World that Vanished......................24

Chapter 5 — Finally 35

Introduction

This is the story of my personal inner journey, which I took with the guidance of unseen teachers. I sensed that these teachers were invariably on my right-hand side. As a rule, I did not see them, but I heard them speaking to me. Although our conversations were in my mind, I heard them clearly and precisely, word for word. This inner journey was a revelation to me. It completely changed my life in a very good way.

The Loving Road to Truth tells the story of an inner journey I experienced in 1978, when I was forty-one years old, that took about five years to complete. The first four chapters describe the four phases I experienced on this journey. The first phase, "Letting Go," covered the releasing of beliefs and the oneness of creation. The second phase, described in chapter 2, took me to a completely different understanding of reincarnation. Chapter 3 took me into the depth, power, and meaning of unconditional love. The last chapter describes my journey into the illusion of manifestation and the world.

It has taken me nearly forty years to write about my journey into truth. I realized when I first had my inner journey in the 1970s that my experiences were very different from the spiritual beliefs held by most spiritually minded people at that time. Although I have written my story as my personal experience, I was always aware that many people had taken this journey before me, and many people will tread the same path after me. For me to have taken this journey, very simply, was motivated by the deep desire for truth, absolute truth, and the wisdom to understand it.

I was born in England in the maternity hospital facing the houses of Parliament, as were my three brothers. This should have been auspicious, except for the fact that I was born two years before the outbreak of war with Germany. We children spent our young lives in the Anderson shelter at the end of the garden, during the horror of the blitz. I was eight years old when peace was finally declared. This beginning taught me not to expect too much in life. Once I made it to adulthood, life changed for the better. I married a good husband and was blessed with a lovely son.

My hope is that you find something in my story that will inspire you to find your inner wisdom and to become aware of your teachers, guides, and helpers.

Prior to taking this journey, I had been a spiritual healer for about three years. I was drawn to healing by my own ill health. I had a scan on the lump in my throat and was told I had a goiter with five nodules attached to it. Despite the goiter, I was told the thyroid was still functioning normally, and it was better to leave things alone. My sister-in-law suggested I go to a spiritual healer she recommended. I visited the healer weekly for a few months. Although the healer was unhappy that he was unable to heal me, he had enabled me to discover my own gift for healing.

Until my visit to the healer, I had never heard of spiritual healing. There was a small group of women who greeted his clients and offered them tea and cakes. These women talked about everything spiritual. They spoke about their experiences as mediums and about miraculous healings. They described their spiritual guardians. I was interested in the healing. They told me that everyone could develop the gift of healing.

After my healing session, I drove home and practiced the laying on of hands on my dear old dog, Sindy. The following week, when I arrived for my healing session, the healer looked at me and said, "I see you have been practicing healing." I confessed I had been practicing on my dog. With his amazing insight, I guessed he already knew that. He encouraged me to join the National Federation of Spiritual Healers (NFSH) as a trainee healer. He also said that I should look for a healing group nearer to my home and ask them if I could join as a trainee healer.

I took his advice and joined the NFSH as a trainee healer. When I went to my first federation weekend, I was invited to practice healing on a full-member healer. He sat on a chair, and I was told to stand behind him. As I laid my hands on his shoulders, I began to feel pulses of energy in my hands and fingers and a powerful energy on top of my head. He was impressed with the healing he felt and said that I should apply for full membership with the federation. That same weekend, I was invited to join a group of healers nearer my home.

A few months later, I became a full member of the NFSH. Although I was now a healer, I was still in awe of the energies awakened in me. I was hungry for knowledge. I wanted to know and understand the mysteries of healing and spirituality.

So I was now a member of the NFSH, had joined a couple of healing groups, and attended the federation's healing weekends. I was the proverbial sponge, soaking up everything as I went along. It was all so new to me. I had been shown the rudiments of healing, and the rest was down to intuition. My intuition showed me where to lay my hands. Powerful energies flowed through me, and released through my hands, healing happened. The notion I had of me doing the healing was gradually to change over time.

During that time, I also attended spiritual symposiums. I listened to many speakers and attended many workshops. I bought their books and listened to their lectures. The more I read and listened, the more difficult I found it to separate the wheat from the chaff. There were so many conflicting ideas. But this was the new age, the Age of Aquarius, and I was swept along with all the enthusiasm and vitality that surrounded me.

When I was doing the healing, I began seeing doctors from the other side of life attend to the people who had asked me for healing. On other occasions, I saw nursing nuns offer their healing to the sick. Another time, when I was healing a young woman who chose to sit on a chair in her bedroom for the healing, I saw three men enter the room. I knew they were doctors. I moved a step backward as the three doctors bent toward the young woman. Then I saw the room fill with onlookers. They all seemed to be trying to see the doctors at work. I again moved backward, until finally, my back was pressed against the wall. As I stood there watching, I realized that I was surplus to requirements. It wasn't my healing energies that did the healing. The healing came from the doctors, surgeons, and specialists from the other side of life, who decided to continue practicing medicine here.

Although I felt redundant on that occasion, there were times when the healers from the other dimension showed me what they were doing. On one occasion, the person who asked for healing was suffering with cancer. I became aware of three chimneys standing upright on the person's abdomen. I noticed black dust particles coming out of those chimneys. I asked what the black particles were. I was told they were the consciousness of the growths, which had been persuaded to leave. When the consciousness left the growth, the growth died. The healer explained to me that the consciousness of the growths was within the consciousness of the person. So really, it was the person, not the healer, who released the consciousness of the growths.

I carried on working with the healing groups for a few more months, I visiting people unable to leave their homes for healing. During one of those visits, I learned the importance of keeping one of the laws of healing: always make sure the individual asked for healing himself or herself. The wife of a very sick man asked me to visit her husband to give him healing. For some reason, it had always been my practice to ask the individual I was to work on if he or she would like healing. On that occasion, the man's wife insisted that he wanted it. Although I sat with him for some time, the healing didn't flow. I told him I was sorry that the healing hadn't flowed. He said he had told his wife he did not want any healing, but she ignored his wishes and asked me to come. His wife apologized to me for going against her husband's wishes. I hugged his wife before I left. It was such a sad case of a desperate wife wanting her husband to be well.

I began to feel uneasy working with the healing groups. I was confused by all the contradictory beliefs concerning spirituality. I felt that I needed time to think and sort out all the conflicting ideas. I knew it was time for me to move on. I was sorry to leave the groups. It took some time to persuade my friends that I really needed to leave. I knew that I had to leave in order to find myself.

I gave myself time to think. I knew without a doubt that I did not want any more confusion in my life regarding spirituality. What I really wanted was just the truth, the absolute truth, and the inner wisdom to understand it. This became my mantra. All I want is absolute truth and the inner wisdom to understand it.

Within a few days, I became aware of the presence of my unseen teachers. I realized they were not new to me. They had been with me when I was a child. I had heard them speaking to me whenever I needed guidance. A teacher at junior school had urged us all to listen to the voice of our consciences in order to lead good lives. For some time, I believed those voices were from my conscience, but the help I was given was always beyond my own awareness, something I could not have known myself. As I grew into adulthood, those voices continued to help me in difficult times. Oddly enough, I realized I never asked for help. My teachers always seemed to be with me. When I felt lost or lonely, or had fallen down a black hole, they showed me how to climb out of my misery.

So those wonderful teachers were with me again, but absolute truth and inner wisdom to know the truth was a tall order. I was told the first thing I needed to understand and keep in mind was that I had to bring everything I experienced on a spiritual level into my intellect, so I would be able to express the experience in simple words.

Chapter 1

Letting Go

Although I realized that these teachers, whose voices I heard very clearly, were unseen by me, I knew that in their realm, they were normal people, still living their lives as we do here in this realm. When, on rare occasions, I glimpsed the other world, I was always amazed by its staggering beauty. The people from that realm who stepped forward to teach me were obviously enlightened.

I had no idea at the beginning of my introduction to the teachers that I was going to be taken on what I would describe as a spiritual inner journey of enlightenment. With hindsight, I realized the teachers had a definite plan of action.

I became aware of my teacher when, one day, I was

remembering my first job with the bank and realized women were paid a third less than men on the same grade. I was angry and resentful at this inequality. She joined me in my memory and showed me how that experience created a belief pattern that colored the whole of my life. This was the first belief I was encouraged to discard. I realized that my beliefs, when scrutinized by my teacher and held up in front of me, enabled me to see I needed to abandon that belief. I found it very easy to let go of my no longer needed beliefs. I was helped to realize eventually that I didn't hold a single belief that came under the category of truth, let alone absolute truth. This meant, of course, everything I had absorbed or learned since my birth from my parents, siblings, schoolteachers, friends, newspapers, magazines, radio, and television. Every belief I had adopted or created for myself had to be released. All the beliefs I held about England and other nations were untrue. Beliefs I hadn't known I had surfaced and had to be released. In the beginning, these beliefs came to light when, for example, I thought of a friend and decided exactly what she should do to solve her problem. I was very good at telling people how to live their lives. I thought I was helping them to be happy. My teacher would join me in my reverie and point out the error of that belief. It wasn't my business to tell people how to live their lives. It was up to them to live their lives in their own ways. I was happy to abandon that ghastly belief. I was told I must realize that creation as I knew it was perfection. Somewhere deep inside me, I knew this was true, but my intellect would not take it. So I asked my teacher, "What about the SS man who picked up the child by his feet and smashed his head against the wall? Tell me, where is the perfection in that?"

My teacher replied, "What you have to realize is that you do not know what the SS man and the child were working out together. It is not for you to judge the actions of other people. It is none of your business. Something you need to understand is that everything that happens in this creation happens exactly as it is meant to."

At that time, I was also having what I would call "teaching dreams." I awoke one morning with the memory of a vivid dream. In the dream, I saw two grown men viciously fighting. I thought they would end up killing each other. I decided to get into the middle and stop them from fighting. As I tried to get to them, something like a glass wall prevented me from reaching them. I watched in horror at what might happen to them. They changed into two small animals. These animals carried on the fight, but after a while, they seemed to tire of fighting and in accord, separated. They shook themselves and walked away completely unharmed.

The same morning, I was still thinking about that strange dream when I went down to the living room and opened the doors leading outside to the patio. As I walked on to the patio, I was upset to see a mass of feathers under the magnolia tree. I knew they had belonged to the woodpigeon who frequently visited our garden. I guessed that one of our neighbor's cats had killed the woodpigeon. I immediately found myself thinking, *If only I had come downstairs an hour earlier, I could have shooed the cat away and saved the bird's life.*

Then I heard my teacher speak to me. "Would you deny the bird and the cat their experiences?" Put like that, there was nothing I could say. I now understood why I was not able to intervene with the men fighting in my dream. Would I have denied the men their experiences? That particular belief I had held—that it was all right for me to interfere with other people's lives, even though I thought I was being helpful—was another belief to release. When I knew that a belief no longer served me, it was like discarding clothes that no longer fit.

My thoughts on morality and immorality had to be released. I had read in the newspaper that a member of Parliament with a wife and young family was caught on camera dining out with his mistress, whom he maintained in a flat in London. There was a public outcry at the appalling immorality of this man, which I agreed with. I was shown that by thinking this man was immoral was just a disguise for judgement. I was judgmental about the way he was living his life. I didn't think he should live his life his way. He wasn't obeying my rules. This was one more horrid belief of mine I was pleased to be rid of. After all, who was I to judge perfection? A perfect creation, that was working out exactly as it was meant to.

I was not sure how long it took me to abandon my beliefs. I was unaware of time. I was aware of my teacher bringing my attention to my beliefs. I became faster at recognizing the problems with my beliefs, and it was easier to dismiss them and let them go. I was still busy with running the home, shopping, and preparing the evening meal for my husband and son. Most of my teaching went on when I sat down with a cup of tea in the afternoon.

I was releasing all my beliefs with the help of my teachers, who were bringing my beliefs forward for me to acknowledge them. I think anyone who wants to release their own beliefs could begin by asking themselves what beliefs they hold that they wish they didn't have. I think once you start looking at your beliefs and your attention is focused, more and more of your beliefs come to your attention. You can then decide if those beliefs do you or anybody else any good. If you do not like your beliefs, throw them out; get rid of them.

My Beliefs Have Gone; I No Longer Exist

Very gradually, I was releasing my beliefs, one after another, until one day it dawned on me that I no longer existed. I realized there was nothing left of me. All the beliefs I had held, which had given me my personality, had been released. I realized I had been peeled like an onion, slowly, layer by layer, until I was aware there was just a minute piece in the center of the onion that remained. As I acknowledged it, that last piece of the onion disappeared. As that last remnant of me disappeared, I saw in my mind's eye an enormous hourglass. I realized I was briefly in the top section of that hourglass, without any sand. I slid down into all the sand at the bottom of the hourglass. I knew that sand was symbolic of the whole of creation. Although by releasing all my beliefs I had become nothing, by falling into the whole of creation, I somehow now knew that I was everything. I was absolutely everything. I was one with everything. To experience this oneness, duality had shown me I had to experience becoming nothing by releasing all the beliefs that had given me substance. Then I would be able to experience becoming everything—absolute oneness.

I walked slowly around the house. I was in awe, knowing that I was everything. I became aware of a beam of light that shone into the room from a high window. I noticed the dust particles dancing in that beam. I knew without a doubt that I was the beam of light and the dust particles. I was amazed when I realized the ray of light and the dust particles had the same consciousness I possessed. So I was everything, and everything was me; we all shared the same consciousness. I tried to think of something that wasn't me. It was impossible. The dust particles and I have the same consciousness, the dust particles were me, and I was the dust particles. Together we were oneness.

My mind was suddenly flooded with a distant yet familiar memory of oneness. I realized that I had always known oneness, but I had forgotten that I knew it. I now remembered I had always been in that state of oneness, but I had to become nothing to remember that I was everything. I realized the absolute necessity for duality. Without duality, there would be nothing to remember. Oneness is the opposite of individuality. I, like everybody else, entered this creation to experience individuality, and as an individual, I had experienced everything. I experienced life. I had lived my own life and been aware of the lives of my family and friends. I had also been aware of the lives of millions of other people in my own country and millions more in other countries. I understood happiness; I was aware of wars. I knew what it was like to suffer. I knew the meaning of goodness and about cruelty and evil actions. That was the knowing that gave my individual life meaning. This creation, which had always been crammed with experiences and knowledge, allowed me to know that I was an individual.

Although I was now aware of the total oneness of creation, I still had within me the memory of the individual. When I released all my beliefs, I was reduced to nothingness. It was only my beliefs that had given my individuality substance. The hardest lesson I learned was that creation was perfect and working out exactly as it was meant to. I thought creation needed to change and that it needed my assistance. How wrong I was. I was prone to help people to become as I thought they needed to be to be happy. Now I knew that people need to live their own lives. If someone asked me to help them now, I would be happy to give the individual any help he or she needed. I would not interfere; I would only give the person the specific help asked for.

Knowing oneness changed me. I saw creation in a different light. I knew that whatever happened to anyone happened to me. In every violent act, I was the victim and the aggressor. Because I was both the victim and the aggressor, the act cancelled itself out. How was I to judge anything that happened when I knew that I was everything? I knew that whatever I did to anyone or anything, I did it to myself. I realized that nothing in creation breathed in without me breathing in with it. I knew that oneness included the unseen world. The unseen world and this world intermingle; they share the same space. The only difference between the two worlds is that the unseen world is incredibly beautiful, and there are no banks; cash is not required.

Becoming nothing and losing my individuality, I can no longer be the "I am." Being everything, I can only be the "am." To resurrect I am is to bring back individuality and separation from the oneness.

Chapter 2

Reincarnation: Another Way

I had experienced oneness. I knew that I was everything. I began to think about reincarnation. I reasoned that because I was everything, I must also have been every reincarnation.

I had attended lectures on reincarnation but had not been drawn to the notion of living one life after another. I knew that many spiritual people had a strong belief that everybody lived many lives. It was important for them to live their present lives in an exemplary way so their next lives would be much better. Although I had never been interested in reincarnation, for some reason I now thought of nothing else. I spent time in the local bookshop. I browsed all the books about reincarnation. I chose a couple of books and they were the beginning of a long list that would be my main reading matter for the next two years. The authors approached reincarnation from different angles, but the subject was just the same— one life followed by another, ad infinitum. I wondered why I was not inspired. Some books I read were very large, very dry, and in some cases, unbelievably boring. But I made myself read every word, just in case a single word or a sentence would suddenly inspire and enlighten me. I was amazed how much I read about reincarnation. I constantly pondered the belief of multiple lives following one after another.

One day, I had been sitting quietly, thinking about the book I had just finished, when I heard my unseen teacher's voice say to me, "So do you think you understand reincarnation now?"

"Well, as far as it goes, I understand the technicalities of reincarnation," I replied. I then saw my teacher walk forward from my side. She walked to the center of the rug, and as she did so, I saw on the floor what looked like a large pile of A4 sheets of paper. I realized the pile of paper on the floor was symbolic of the work I had done, studying reincarnation. She bent down, picked up the pile of paper, tore it in half, and tossed it in the air. I thought that was my teacher's way of saying that she had disposed of all that unnecessary work I had done.

"That's good," my teacher said. "Now I can tell you what reincarnation is really all about."

I was aghast. I could not believe that I had studied reincarnation for so long, and it was obviously not right.

I was upset. "I can't believe that you let me waste these past years studying reincarnation if it wasn't right. How could you let me waste my time like that?"

She replied, "Nothing is ever wasted. You needed a sound basic knowledge and understanding of reincarnation to enable me to build on it."

My teacher left. I was in no frame of mind to continue. I was so angry that I had wasted those good years, trying to be inspired and to truly understand reincarnation. Later, my teacher returned. She said, "I want you to think of a piano keyboard. Imagine that the ivories, the white keys, are symbolic of your span of lives. If you press the first key down, this represents your first life. When you lift your finger off the key, this will symbolize the end of that life. Then you press down the next key, which is your next life, and once again, when you lift your finger off the key, this is the end of that life. And so forth along the rest of the keys. This is how you understand reincarnation."

I remarked that every book I read said exactly that. After my interruption, she carried on. "Now I want you to imagine a long baton of wood, long enough to stretch from the first key to the very last one. Imagine placing your hands on that baton of wood. Press the baton down firmly. As you can see, all the keys have gone down together at the same time. This is how the span of your lives happened, all together, instantly. Of course, using the piano keyboard in this way does not give you a very good idea of the true length of your span of lives. When you imagine the keyboard, look to your left and see the keyboard extends as far as you can see; the same applies when looking to the right. To have a truer picture, you would need to see in the distance the curve of the lines on both sides as the line forms a large, perfect circle. Your whole circle of experiences happened instantly. Creation as you know it was the same. The whole of creation happened instantly. You could say, spiritually speaking, that creation happened in one day. The whole of life happened at once." I wanted to interrupt her, but she continued speaking.

"You think of life as being governed by linear time. You see life in terms of the past, the present, and the future. Life was never linear; it was instantaneous. All life happened at once, so what you must realize, of course, is that creation, as you know it, has been and gone. It began and it ended."

At this point, I interrupted my teacher. My mind disregarded the last sentences, much to my chagrin later. I was fascinated by the thought that all life happened at once, and as I seem to still be living in this life, I asked, "If all life happened at once, does that mean the pharaohs must be alive and living at the same time as me?" I knew Egyptian mummies had been taken from their tombs and that some were unwrapped. I had seen one in the museum.

My teacher answered, "What you have to realize is that someone at this moment could be digging up your bones." So the pharaohs were dead, as I knew they were. I am also dead, as dead as the pharaohs. But how can I be dead? I think I am still alive. If all life happened instantly, rather than happens instantly in the present context, it is obvious that creation as I know it has been and gone. Life began and ended.

So I understood. Rather than the idea of a linear belief that I lived one life after another, now I had the notion that all of life happened at once, and consequently, creation as I know it, which my teacher always emphasized to me, has been and gone. It began and it ended. This creation, as I know it, appears to me to be real. But since it does not exist, what is it that I, and everyone and everything else, are experiencing at this moment? Is this just a flashback of memory? Are we all just a memory? Now, at last I understood what was meant when I was told that everything is thought. Everything is within the mind of the massive consciousness.

Many years ago, I asked my teacher if there was a god. She didn't answer my question, but she told me a story to help me understand the answer to my question. She told me about the lonely child who imagined a playmate, a friend. This friend was very real to him, and when the boy's mother called him to the table for lunch, he would not eat until his mother provided lunch for his friend. He and his friend chatted away while they ate their lunches, but the mother was aware the friend's food was congealing on the plate. This little story was given to me to emphasize the origin of creation. Like the lonely boy who imagined his friend, we are the imagined companions held within the imagination of the massive conscious awareness, which also knew absolute loneliness. And as a result, that huge mind imagined a whole creation of companions.

When the little boy slept, did he forget his imaginary

friend? When he awakened in the morning, did he immediately remember his little imagined friend? How was it with the massive thinking conscious awareness? Was the instantaneous creation constantly remembered? How many times has this creation repeated itself? How is it that when I experienced oneness, I knew I had always known oneness, but for some reason had forgotten that I knew it? How many times have I been down this same road? I expect many people experience those flashes of cognition when they know what the future holds for them in those moments of clear sight. The future we see must already be there in place, must already have been written and performed.

The imagined friend of the lonely little boy sat at table with him and chatted while they both ate their lunch. So vivid was the boy's imagination that he saw his friend eat. Within the mind of the massive thinking awareness, do we actually eat?

I pondered long and hard on the description that my teacher gave me of the instantaneous span of my lives forming a large and perfect circle. The whole saga of my lives was segmented on that huge circle. I had remembered this segment. At the same time, I remembered all the other segments. Now I understood when I was told that we were all unaware of the many planes of experience that we inhabit at the same time. Although we are all experiencing what we would describe as this present life, without realizing it, we are also living the whole span of our lives. All our lives happened at once.

I was reminded of an unusual experience when I

realized I had come up behind myself as a very small child. I asked my teacher what this strange experience meant. She explained that I had completed the circle of personal experience for this life and had started another circle. Later, I realized that the circles were not closed. They were like a spring, running side by side. You can stretch a spring to open it up or flatten it by pressing it together, like a concertina. This is how I see my span of lives, concertinaed on either side of me.

I seemed to spend so much of my life constantly pondering all the things my teachers taught me. I knew the instantaneous reincarnation I had been shown was very different from the linear reincarnation expressed in all the books I read.

My life carried on for some time with no word from my teachers, although I continued to ponder all the aspects of oneness and reincarnation. My teachers had not deserted me; they were waiting for me.

Chapter 3

What Is This Thing Called Love?

The most difficult part of my inner journey took me into the realms of love. Deep down, I had always felt I was unloved. I managed to suppress these feelings. Although eventually, I was to learn if one suppresses an emotion, it will inevitably surface later with a force that can be frightening. I knew my childhood had not been a loving one. I realized that a vow I'd made when I was eleven years old was the final nail in my coffin. This vow created an everlasting lack of love within me.

After the war, my parents separated. My mother, two of my brothers, and I moved to the flat upstairs. My eldest brother, Bernard, and father lived downstairs. This way of living went on for three years, until my mother packed her bags to leave. She stood her cases by the front door in readiness of leaving and waited for my father to return from work. As he came in, she stopped him at the bottom of the stairs. She had already told me to stay upstairs. She placed mine and my young brother's ration books on the filial at the bottom of the stairs and said to my father, "I am leaving, and you can look after them now."

My father replied, "I don't want them. They are your responsibility. You can get back up those stairs, and get on with it,"

Mother said, "I don't want them either. Now you can have a basin full of them." I stood at the top of the stairs, watching them argue over who wasn't going to have us. Eventually, my mother picked up her cases and left. As the front door closed behind her, I felt an unbearable pain in my chest and knew my heart had been torn apart. I vowed that nobody would ever do this to me again. Nobody would ever be allowed into my heart again. Although I was only eleven years old when I made that vow, it stayed with me, and with my heart shuttered in steel, love could not enter; nor could love be given. Although by adulthood I had forgotten that vow, it was obviously still intact and proved to be very costly. As an adult, I thought I loved and was loved, like everybody else. But something was never quite right inside me. This unease did not have a name.

Many years later, I asked one of my teachers why I stood at the top of those stairs and watched my mother leave. Why hadn't I run down the stairs, grab her by the ankles, and beg her to take me with her? My teacher answered, "If one iota of your life had been different, you would not be where you are today."

During the time I was experiencing the teachings that were taking me on my internal journey, a friend asked me to attend a spiritual workshop she was organizing. I drove up to the north of Yorkshire and stayed with her for the week. When I drove home, the weather had worsened, and snow and sleet slowed traffic. I eventually arrived home at about four o'clock in the afternoon. As I looked out the kitchen window, there was only about four inches of snow, and a mass of tightly budded daffodils were peeping just above the snow line. I went out and picked a huge bunch. I arranged them in a china swan and placed them on the mantelpiece.

After dinner that evening, my husband went to bed early because his colleague was going to pick him up at four o'clock in the morning for an early flight to Germany. That morning, my birthday, I came down alone for breakfast. Propped behind an ornament on the mantelpiece was a birthday card from my husband. He hadn't left a present for me, not even a bunch of flowers. I had been away for a week. However busy he had been, he must have had plenty of time to buy me something, for my birthday. I was very upset about this. I reasoned that he didn't love me enough to leave a present for me. *I really don't think that he loves me at all. Why doesn't he love me?*

Then I heard my teacher's voice. "Love does not exist outside yourself; love comes from within."

I replied, "I don't want love to come from within. I want to be loved."

My teacher answered, "There is no love to be found outside yourself; love comes from within."

I tried another tactic. "I just want to be loved."

Again came the gentle calm voice. "There is no love out there. You will never find love outside yourself. Love is not out there. Love comes from within."

I shouted at my teacher, who clearly didn't understand, "I know there is love out there. Everybody looks for love out there, and that's what I want."

Again that gentle insistence of my teacher. "You will never find love outside yourself. How can you find something that does not exist? Love comes from within."

I was losing heart, but I tried again. "If my husband doesn't love me enough to leave me a present, at least he could have left me a bunch of flowers."

My teacher's calm voice answered me, "If you want flowers, you must supply them for yourself. And look, you have."

I looked up at the mantelpiece, and there was the mass of tightly budded daffodils I picked from the garden the previous day. They were in full bloom. They looked beautiful, but I was not surrendering. "I don't care about the daffodils. I don't want to supply my own flowers. I want my husband to think enough about my birthday to have at least left me some flowers. He doesn't even love me enough to leave me a bunch of flowers."

Once again, I hear the gentle voice of my long-suffering teacher. "Love comes from within. You will never find it anywhere else."

I am frustrated. I do not know what my teacher means.

How can love only come from within? My teacher has worn me down, and I was tearful. I got up and opened the doors to the patio. I took a chair with me and sat outside. A weak sun was melting what was left of the remaining snow. It was no longer cold, and the sun warmed me. I was upset and weepy. I made a mountain out of a molehill and argued the toss with my teacher. All to no avail. What on earth does it mean, "Love comes from within"? How can love only come from within?

Then it happened. I felt myself drop right down deep inside my body. I had fallen into myself, into this massive love. This massive love was so huge, I felt that it must be larger than the whole of the universe. This love was completely besotted with me. I was adored. With this absolute love, I knew I did not need any other sort of love. I was made of this love. Every cell in my body was made of this love. There was not a single atom of me that was not made of this love. I was this love. I was nothing else. I was just this pure love. I wallowed in this joyous ecstasy of love.

I realized that this amazing love had no side to it. It did not judge or find any fault with me. I realized that I could be a mass murderer, but this love would not have changed toward me in any way. This love just was. It was complete, whole, and pure. I looked down at my body and saw I was still my same shape. How was it that this love inside me was more massive than the universe? I knew I was the whole of this universal love. I knew I was not just a speck of it. Nor was I just an individual piece. I was it, the whole of that universal love. There was nothing else other than this massive universal love. It dawned on me that everything else in creation knew they were the whole of that enormous universal love. Not just humans, but an ant on the ground, a cockroach, a single leaf on a tree knew they were that whole universal love.

I became aware that this amazing massive universal love had no knowledge of itself and was completely unconscious and unaware of its own existence. This love was absolutely and completely in a state of unknowing. This love was not conscious.

It was as though once I understood this universal love did not know it existed, was without knowledge, and in a state of unknowing that I suddenly saw this love completely wrapped around with all knowing. My intellect flooded up from the depths, and I found myself thinking, *Quickly, quickly. This is "all knowing." Ask it that question that has been bothering you.* But it dawned on me that I, and everybody, were the all-knowing, so it was pointless to ask questions. Although I knew I was the all-knowing, I was not very sure what I actually knew. I then realized what this all knowing really was. It was the total of what every human being, every animal, insect, mineral, and vegetable already knew about this imagined life, this creation, that had allowed us to experience knowledge and the awareness to know we existed. We had all experienced this life, the all-knowing.

Without this life that I had lived and the awareness I gained from having experienced this life, the all-knowing would have been impossible to have known and acknowledged the unknowing absolute love everybody, the whole of creation, is made from. Without this duality of the all-knowing (life) and the unknowing (unconditional love), I would never have been able to acknowledge the source, the very core of my being, this absolute love.

Later that day, I answered the door to our local florist. She presented me with a beautiful bouquet of flowers. She apologized for bringing them to me so late in the day. She explained that her assistant was off sick that day, and she was not able to do her deliveries until after she closed her shop. These lovely flowers were from my husband, wishing me a happy birthday. How fortunate for me that these flowers arrived so late. Had they arrived early in the morning, as they should have been, I would not have had my amazing experience with unconditional love.

This massive love from which we are all made is spoken of as unconditional love. As such, it has nothing to do with our notion of physical love. We are generally taught to ration physical love to those people we love, and the people we do not like have none of our love. When I fell into this massive inner love, my whole outlook on life changed. This unconditional love was so profound, so deep, and so powerful in my life. Having the experience of oneness, and knowing I was everyone and everything, colored my world. I soon noticed this change as I read a newspaper, and there was a picture of a man found guilty of raping and murdering a young girl. I looked in the bewildered eyes of this man and was swamped with love for him. I knew, of course, that most people would look at his picture and despise him for what he had done. But this unconditional love could not judge, and I could no longer go down that road of judgment.

I had to acknowledge that absolute unconditional love cannot be confused with compassion. I saw an elderly lady pushing her shopping basket toward the entrance to the supermarket. She was so unwell. She was bent over her trolley as she pushed it along. Her poor legs were completely swollen, and she obviously had great difficulty walking. I was filled with compassion for her. I felt so sad watching her painful progress, and I asked the spiritual powers for healing for this dear soul. Instantly I heard my teacher say, "You must stop looking at the physical plight of people. You must learn to see them as the beautiful souls that they are." I knew that I should have just loved her. Compassion was not the answer and was of no value to her or me. When I thought about my feeling of compassion for this dear woman, I realized my feelings could have been construed as pity. Who in this world would want to be pitied? Unconditional love, on the other hand, can be felt and appreciated by everyone.

There were so many lessons from my teachers. There was so much for me to learn. On the horizon loomed another lesson for me. It was to be one that would test my sanity.

Chapter 4

The World that Vanished

One afternoon I was sitting in my living room, enjoying a cup of tea and listening to *Woman's Hour* on Radio 4. The next moment, I found myself standing outside the world. I looked down onto planet Earth, and I realized there were no people. I looked closer and saw there were no animals or birds. There was no water of any kind. There were no trees or grass, no plants or greenery of any kind. I realized that planet Earth wasn't there, either. I saw that there was nothing there at all.

I looked to my left, where the sun should have been. The sun wasn't there. I realized that the moon wasn't there, either. There were no stars and no Milky Way. I knew that millions of pounds had been spent observing those stars. I was appalled at what I saw. I reasoned this was a ghastly con trick played on humankind. We all thought we lived on planet Earth. We lived our lives on a beautiful planet, in the company of animals of every kind. We believed the skies were often filled with amazing birds. We thought there were streams, rivers, and oceans filled with fish and all sorts of aquatic life. What about the insect world? We all thought we understood the huge insect world around us. We took beautiful scenery for granted. All those wonderful trees; the grass and plants; fields of corn, wheat, and barley were always in our lives.

Now I knew we had all been deceived. We had been fooled, tricked into believing in a world that did not exist. I was devastated as I stood staring into that void, that nothingness. I knew that I, the observer, was still there. I looked at that emptiness and realized I had to return to that void. There was nowhere else for me to go. With that realization, I was returned to my home.

My life continued exactly as it always had. I carried on with the usual chores. I washed, ironed, cleaned, shopped, and socialized with friends. Overriding all that activity, I knew without a doubt that the life I lived was, in fact, a lie. How could I have lived any sort of life on a planet Earth that did not exist? The sun that warmed me, the moon that shone in the night sky, the myriad stars that I had marveled at were not there, either. They simply did not exist for me when I was taken by my teacher to the outside of the world and saw it for myself.

Here I was at home, doing all the things I did before.

I could see the sun in the sky. At night, the moon and the stars still shone in the night sky.

These conflicting thoughts haunted me, and I thought about nothing else. I awakened in the morning with those thoughts. They were with me all day. At night, they were with me until sleep gave me a few hours of peace. My mind was in turmoil. I could not rationalize my experience of a universe that did not exist with my life that obviously continued. That internal struggle began to take a toll on me, and I became very depressed. On the outside, I put on a brave face and appeared cheerful and positive. But inside, I had fallen into a black pit of misery. I feared that I was very quietly going completely insane.

My unseen teachers had given me so many clues about nothingness. During the time, I had been shown how reincarnation really happened. I came to understand that my line of experiential lives all happened instantly at the same time, and creation as I knew it had been and gone, begun and ended. To emphasize how instantaneous creation had been, my teacher told me to imagine myself in a shooting gallery and to take aim at the target with a gun. I imagined myself lifting my arm straight in front of me, and I squeezed the trigger and fired. Instantly, the bullet hit the target. My teacher had said, "Spiritually speaking, that is what instantaneous means." My teacher could not have made it clearer that creation had instantly begun and instantly ended. It is so difficult to understand that concept.

My father told me of an occasion when he used the public swimming pool. He had dived from the top board and hit the water badly. His whole body went into cramp, and in agony, he sank to the bottom of the pool. He thought he was going to die. He said his whole life flashed through his mind in precise detail. Had creation flashed through the great mind in precise detail?

Why had I not grasped the nettle then? Instead, the meaning of instantaneous creation passed me by. My teachers had taken me outside the world to make me see for myself what nothingness really meant. I still could not understand how we were all carrying on with our lives, regardless of this nothingness.

I knew, of course, that everything was thought. I also understood that creation was instantaneous and within the imagination of a massive, aware consciousness. But I always had to return to this life, this life that appeared to be happening inside nothingness.

I saw a weekend workshop advertised in Sir George Trevelyan's *Wrekin Trust* program. I knew I had to attend that workshop. I was too late with my booking to secure a residential place, but I was able to book as a daily attendee. The workshop was to be held in Sunbury-on-Thames, which was only an hour and a half drive from my home. As things turned out, this was a perfect arrangement for me.

I arrived early on that first day of the workshop. I checked in and made my way to the lounge, where I intended to sit and wait for the first lecture of that day. The residents who had arrived the previous evening were still having breakfast in the dining room next to the lounge. Seated at the far end of the lounge, on one of the large sofas, were two saffron-robed monks. I walked toward them, and when I reached them, I asked if I might join them. I could not believe that I asked to join them. Normally, I would have sat somewhere on my own, but for some reason, I just kept on walking toward them. They politely invited me to sit with them. We introduced ourselves. The senior monk was the Venerable Sumedho. I did not catch the name of the much-younger, quiet-spoken monk. In the pause that ensued, I asked the Venerable Sumedho if he was well. He told me he was very well. Another pause, and he asked me how I was. I was just about to say that I was very well, thank you, but instead I heard myself blurt out, "Actually, I am not too good."

He said that he was sorry to hear that, and did I want to tell him what was troubling me? Without a pause for breath, I related my tale of going outside the world and finding that nothing existed. I finished by saying I thought this was the biggest con trick ever played on humankind, to which he replied, "We monks prefer not to call it a 'con trick' but, rather, an illusion." I agreed that "illusion" was a better word to use. As I finished my tale of woe, I mentioned to him that I thought I might be losing my mind.

He suddenly began to laugh, but I was close to tears, thinking I might be losing my mind. He went on laughing heartily for a while, and I began to think that he thought my story was laughable. Then he said, "There is nothing wrong with you. You are not losing your mind. You are in Nirvana, and we monks spend our lives meditating and chanting to be where you are."

I could not believe what he was saying. *And anyway,* I thought, *what on earth is Nirvana?* I said, "You want to be where I am? You must be mad. I am in hell."

The Venerable Sumedho leaned over to his case, which was on the floor beside him, and drew out a thin laminated card that concertinaed out into eight identical squares. These squares were printed with identical circles, and each circle had a different picture inside it. He explained to me that the monks followed an eightfold path, which was represented in those pictures inside the circles. He told me what each picture represented. There were six pictures, and as he described each one to me, I understood their meaning very clearly because I experienced each step. The seventh circle was empty. It represented the nothingness I experienced and was described as Nirvana. I assumed Nirvana was the name for nothingness. The picture in the eighth circle he described as going back into the marketplace. I asked, "How would I be able get back into the marketplace?" He thought for a little while and then said I would find a way.

I thanked the Venerable Sumedho for his help. He had reassured me that I was not in danger of losing my mind because of the strange experience I had when I found myself outside the vanished world and experienced the nothingness. I spent that weekend listening to the wise talks given by the Venerable Sumedho. I hoped he would talk about the world not existing and the nothingness that he had explained to me was a desirable state for the monks. I hoped he would enlarge on the illusion of this life, which appeared to continue inside that nothingness.

But his lectures had already been prepared. Nevertheless, I listened to his wise words, and his assurance that I had not lost my mind gave me some peace. I felt uplifted.

In hindsight, I had found my way back into that marketplace. But I was never fooled by the marketplace because I always viewed it from the seventh circle, the empty circle, the nothingness with a name: Nirvana.

Eventually, I understood why there was only one place for me to go when I realized the world did not exist. I thought I had to go back to that nothingness, to a world that wasn't there. Like everybody else, I thought I lived in a manifested world in a manifested body. I knew, of course, that everything was thought and that we were the imagined creation within the massive conscious awareness, and this, of course, was where we had always been.

I had to go back yet again to the lonely boy and his imaginary friend. This friend who only the boy could see, this friend within his mind, his imaginary friend, the friend who could never manifest. I thought I had to return to a world that did not exist. But instead, I had returned to the creation within the massive consciousness, where I had always been, where this world we all inhabit resides within the imagination of the great mind. Just like the lonely boy in the story. It is the same for us for the whole of creation is imagined by the great consciously aware mind and not manifested.

The last phase I experienced when I was shown the complete absence of the world—the nothingness—was the hardest one for me to understand. Until that moment, with every experience I had, every moment when the light bulb went on in my mind or the penny dropped, and I felt the awe of enlightenment, my second thought was that I always knew that but had forgotten it. The truth is that we all already know everything but have chosen not to remember.

I was not afraid of the nothingness; it was the absence of the world that threw me. I had experienced complete nothingness some years before, when I was doing healing. A friend asked me to give her some healing at the end of a group session, just before we were to leave for home. I laid my hands on the table and asked her to place hers on top of mine. She closed her eyes, and I closed mine. The next moment, I found myself inside an enormous sphere. I realized there was nothing inside this sphere, not even a chair or a book. Yet I knew that I would like to stay in this sphere forever. There was nothing to commend this sphere. Inside, there wasn't any light; nor was there any darkness. There was just pure nothingness. I wanted to be in there forever. But I knew that I could not stay; I had to drive home. I moved toward the inner wall of the sphere, but the wall moved away from me, causing a bulge in the sphere. Then I saw the sphere reshape itself. I knew that if I had the instruments for measuring a sphere, I would find this sphere was perfect. I moved a few more times toward the inner wall. Each time, the same thing happened. The sphere seemed to be complete, without any opening. I knew I was bound by this sphere of nothingness, and there was no way out of it. I knew I was in the core of nothingness—the primal state, before consciousness and awareness arose. I knew this nothingness was the ultimate perfection. This was an experience to be remembered as I opened my eyes and found myself back in the room with my friend.

Had I been able to ask consciousness and awareness, "How did you arise?" neither consciousness nor awareness would have been able to tell me. However, without the occurrence of this phenomenon, the original primal state of nothingness would not have known itself. That conscious mind's awareness was now able to acknowledge the isolation that existed within that massive mind. Using a vivid imagination, the whole of the universe was created within that incredible, consciously aware mind.

I always believed that the imagined creation manifested into physical matter. I thought I lived on the manifested planet Earth. I knew that everything in creation was pure thought. I knew I was held within the imagination of that great mind. That massive, aware, conscious mind was the imagined creation. That creative mind was the sole performer, so the memory of oneness I experienced was of this one massive mind that was everything. I knew creation was instantaneous and that it began and promptly ended. Yet here I was, enmeshed in this creation. Even when I went outside the world and was shown that there was nothing there, I thought I still had to come back to that nothingness, the world that did not exist. That was my conundrum, a contradiction in terms. My teachers were showing me that nothing ever manifested. The manifested world I thought I lived in did not exist; there was nothing there. I was not for real. I was not manifested. I was imagined, and although creation was instantaneous, the memory of that vividly imagined creation remained engraved within the mind of the great consciousness, and as such, I was constantly remembered.

The indigenous Aborigines of Australia called their world "the dream world." When I dreamed, whether it was a good dream or a nightmare, the next morning I knew it was only a dream, and none of that dream really happened. It was probably much easier to have understood living in a dream world than to know I was the imagined creation within the mind of the massive conscious awareness.

An unusual experience that I had reminded me of the Aborigines' belief in the dream world. Although at the time I was standing at the sink, peeling potatoes for our evening meal, I suddenly had the experience of waking up from an eternal dream. I knew that everybody else was still asleep inside the dream. I was filled with grief as I experienced my absolute isolation. I then realized I had awakened inside the eternal dream. There was no escape from that dream. There was nowhere else to go. I quickly concluded there was nothing worse than being awake in your own dream. Eventually, everyone and everything will have to wake up.

I thought I had to return to a world that did not exist. If only I had realized I was returning to that vividly imagined creation held within the great mind. I had always been there, within that great mind of the massive consciousness, where manifestation never happened. There, where that vivid imagined creation abounded with planets galore and a beautiful earth, just as I had always known it. I lived inside that imagined life filled with the experiences that created the imagined "all knowing" to shine a light on the "unknowing" unconditional love and the primordial nothingness.

My teachers wanted me to understand the illusion of our world. My experiences convinced me of the illusion. Knowing that the world is an illusion is good to know, but in truth, nothing has changed. To all of us, the world is still as it has always been, crammed with experiences revealed through the power of duality.

I had no idea where my need for truth was going to take me. I was blessed with determined teachers, but many seekers of truth find it through meditation, by going within to find their own inner wisdom. That amazing inner wisdom has always known the truth.

Chapter 5

Finally

My hope is that you have found the story of my spiritual inner journey of interest. Whether you have experienced a similar inner journey or your experience is completely different than mine, I hope you will find something pertinent to your life.

When I experienced my inner journey, I thought I had gone as far as I could go. I now realize that my story was just the tip of the iceberg. I am forever intrigued by the extraordinary miracle of consciousness and awareness having arisen. Without this amazing miracle, there would be no stories to tell. There would be nothing to remember, and the primordial nothingness would be unaware of its own existence.

I took my inner journey forty years ago. I didn't write down or record a single word of my journey. Every experience I had and all the conversations with my unseen teachers were indelibly written within my mind.

The four phases of teaching I experienced took me on a road to illumination. By releasing my beliefs, I surrendered my individuality to know oneness. Another view of reincarnation showed me how the span of my lives all happened instantly at the same time, as did creation. Unconditional love, profound and incapable of judgment, flooded through me, and judgment left me. The disappearance of the world made me acknowledge my residence within the massive mind of the aware consciousness and the illusion of a manifested creation.

Since my inner journey, I have lived what I thought of as a regular life, at least on the surface. But my journey completely changed me. I couldn't go back to believing in a regular world. It was my inner world that sustained me. My teachers have never deserted me, and I learned the importance of asking questions. Without questions, there can be no answers. I have realized there is no end to spiritual knowledge. The more I learned about the spirituality of creation, the more aware I was of the great depth of knowledge that was still unknown to me.

For as many people that there are in this creation, there are as many ways to enlightenment. Many books have been written about inner enlightenment that can be helpful to those who seek it. The seeker, though, can often experience the desired enlightenment by going within to experience his or her personal inner wisdom. Nobody has the monopoly on enlightenment. Nobody can say his or her way to enlightenment is the only true way. It can be helpful to remember that every journey we take—whether good, bad, or indifferent—is always perfection.

I remember being told the story of a grieving man, weeping as he walked through some snow-covered woods. He caught sight of something green in the snow. He bent down to look at it and saw that it was a delicate green plant with a tiny white flower that managed to push up through the snow. As he reached out and touched it, he was suddenly filled with joy as he realized that he had become fully enlightened. Enlightenment comes in many guises. I often thought about this fortunate man as I struggled with my inner journey. There is one marvelous truth that may help you on your inner journey: We already know everything, and we are already completely enlightened. All we must do is remember it.

During the forty years since my inner journey, I continued asking questions. I have realized that spirituality can never be generalized. A simple question can sometimes raise a very complicated answer. Other answers were given to me by my teachers, taking me to different places to see and experience actual incidents that answered my questions. My inner life continues to flourish, and I am continually reminded of the amazing miracle of conscious awareness we all share.

One final thought. A deep learning curve for me has been the realization that I can't blame anyone or anything for what happens to me. I am the creator of my own life. Everything is down to me. Everything that happens to me

Doris Fouracre

is of my own choosing and is prewritten on the blueprint I carry within me that enables me to satisfy my need for experiencing knowledge. At the same time, I am also aware of the equal truth on the other side of the coin. The great conscious mind, alone, enacts the whole of creation. It is the sole actor, playing all the roles. The one actor, the absolute oneness.

Printed in the United States
By Bookmasters